children's HISTO

THE BLACK COUNTRY

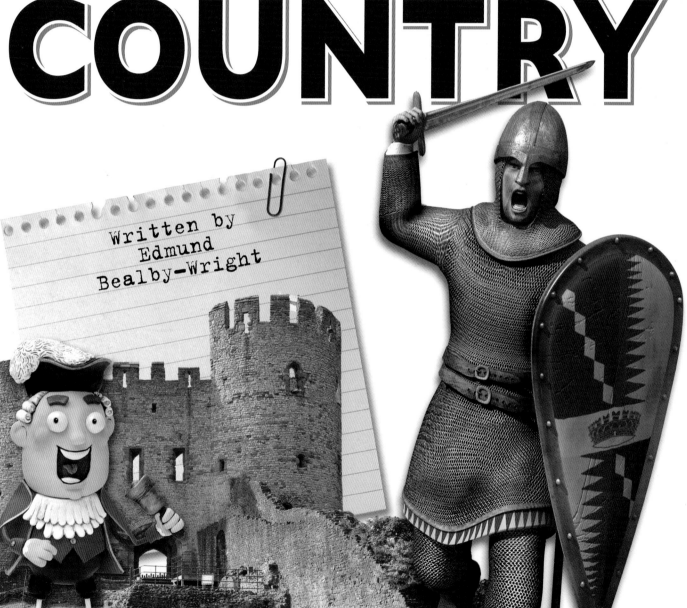

Written by
Edmund
Bealby-Wright

HOMETOWN WORLD

How well do you know your town?

Have you ever wondered what it would have been like living in the Black Country when the Romans arrived? What about meeting Queen Victoria? This book will uncover the important and exciting things that happened in your area.

Want to hear the other good bits? You will love this book! Some rather brainy folk have worked on it to make sure it's fun and informative. So what are you waiting for? Peel back the pages and be amazed at what happened in the Black Country.

Timeline shows which period (dates and people) each spread is talking about

THE FACTS

Invaders

Longships come silently up the river at night. The westerly wind fills their square sails helping them row against the current. They are deep in enemy territory. Each boat is filled with men ready to plunder. The tiller man steers them upstream with an oar carved with the head of a dragon. This was how the Vikings liked to attack – with stealth and extreme violence.

The Battle of Tettenhall

The Vikings were fearless explorers from Scandinavia. They raided Britain stealing, killing anyone who tried to stop them, and taking the treasure back to their ships. But this time they were caught in a trap. On 5th August AD 910 a massive army was waiting for them. There were warriors hiding in the hills and forests near Tettenhall, and they attacked with fury. The Vikings tried to return to the safety of their ships, but their way was blocked. They were surrounded. They had no choice but to face their enemy in battle – and they lost.

Kingdom of Mercia

The victors at the Battle of Tettenhall were the Anglo-Saxons, people from Germany who had invaded and settled here after the Romans left. The Anglo-Saxons divided Angle-Land into small kingdoms, pushing the native Celts westwards. The Black Country was part of the Kingdom of Mercia.

The Black Country was a blanket of green forests and heath, crossed by rough tracks and dotted with tiny clearings. There were waterwheels on the rivers Tame and Stour to power flour mills, and forts such as the stronghold built by a Saxon ruler called 'Dudd', or 'Dodo' in Dudley.

This map shows the kingdoms of Britain in Anglo-Saxon times. Can you see if some names have stayed the same?

Lady Wulfruna

The Vikings were not put off by their defeat at Tettenhall. In AD 943 the Viking leader, Olaf Guthfrithson, led a fierce and bloody attack on Tamworth, which resulted in the capture of Wulfruna, a Saxon noblewoman. She held land and property in her own right on an equal basis to Saxon noblemen. She was also a member of the powerful Mercian ruling family. The Danish Vikings held her to ransom – Olaf knew that Wulfruna was important enough to extract a high price for her release. After, to give thanks, she founded the church in Wolverhampton, where her name is remembered to this day.

Country Life

The Vikings began settling around the Black Country. The old Roman road, Watling Street, became a boundary between Viking parts of England and the Anglo-Saxon kingdom. The Anglo-Saxons became Christians and began to build simple churches, but the old Saxon and Norse gods are still remembered in the days of the week.

A statue of Lady Wulfruna stands outside St Peter's Church, Wolverhampton.

English	Saxon/Norse
Monday	Mona
Tuesday	Tiu
Wednesday	Woden
Thursday	Thor
Friday	Freyja
Saturday	Saeternesdæg
Sunday	Sunne

The English days of the week are named after Saxon and Norse gods.

"Hand over the Danegeld or you don't get Wulfruna back!"

A hoard of Anglo-Saxon gold dug up in a field near Brownhills in 2009 is worth more than £1,000,000!

SPOT THIS! This column is decorated with wild swirling designs carved by Saxons. Can you spot it? Here's a clue – it's not far from St Peter's Church in Wolverhampton.

...AD 606 Anglo-Saxons settle...AD 700 Dudd builds a fort...   *...AD 910 Battle of Tettenhall...AD 943 Wulfruna kidnapped...*

6   7

Clear informative text   *Intriguing old photos*   *'Spot this!' game with hints on something to find in your town*

THE EVIDENCE

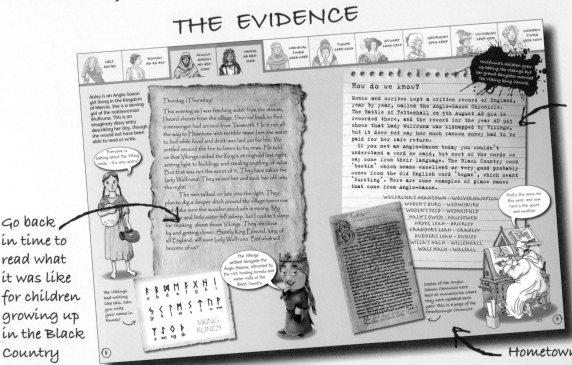

Aisley is an Anglo-Saxon girl living in the Kingdom of Mercia. She is a serving girl of the noblewoman Wulfruna. This is an imaginary diary entry describing her day, though she would not have been able to read or write.

Thordag (Thursday)

This evening as I was fetching water from the stream, I heard shouts from the village. I hurried back to find a messenger had arrived from Tamworth. He'd run all the way to Heantune with terrible news! I set the water to boil while food and drink was laid out for him. We settled around the fire to listen to his news. He told us that Vikings raided the King's stronghold last night, setting light to buildings and stealing anything of value. But that was not the worst of it. They have taken the Lady Wulfruna! They seized her and took her off into the night!

The men talked on late into the night. They plan to dig a deeper ditch around the village tomorrow to make sure the wooden stockade is strong. My brother and little sister fell asleep, but I couldn't sleep for thinking about those Vikings. They are close by and getting closer. Surely King Edmund, king of all England, will save Lady Wulfruna. But what will become of us?

"Everyone is talking about the Viking raids – it's very scary!"

The Vikings settled alongside the Anglo-Saxons, attracted by the rich hunting forests and water mills of the Black Country.

The Vikings had writing like this. Can you write your name in Runes?

VIKING RUNES

How do we know?

Monks and scribes kept a written record of England, year by year, called the Anglo-Saxon Chronicle. The Battle of Tettenhall on 5th August AD 910 is recorded there, and the record for the year AD 943 shows that Lady Wulfruna was kidnapped by Vikings, but it does not say how much ransom money had to be paid for her safe return.

If you met an Anglo-Saxon today you wouldn't understand a word he said, but most of the words we say come from their language. The Black Country word 'bostin' which means excellent or very good probably comes from the Old English word 'bogan', which meant 'bursting'. Here are some examples of place names that come from Anglo-Saxon.

WULFRUNA'S HEANTOWN – WOLVERHAMPTON
WODEN'S BURG – WEDNESBURY
WODEN'S FELD – WEDNESFIELD
HALH'S OWEN – HALESOWEN
HRYCG LEAH – BRIERLEY
CRADDERS LEAH – CRADLEY
DUDDERS LEAH – DUDLEY
WILLA'S HALH – WILLENHALL
WALS HALH – WALSALL

Wulfruna's children grew up hating the Vikings but her grand-daughter married the Viking king Canute.

"That's the news for this year, and now here's the sport and weather."

Copies of the Anglo-Saxon Chronicle were kept at monasteries where they were updated each year. This is a page of the Peterborough Chronicle.

8   9

Go back in time to read what it was like for children growing up in the Black Country

Each period in the book ends with a summary explaining how we know about the past

Hometown facts to amaze you!

Contents

CELT
500 BC

ROMAN
AD 43-410

ANGLO-
SAXON
AD 450-1066

VIKING
AD 865-
1066

MEDIE'
TIME
1066-1

The Romans are Coming!

A young Celtic shepherd is herding his sheep when he hears an amazing rumble coming from the hillside. As far as he can see, a column of soldiers marches along the valley carrying weapons and knapsacks. Behind them come wagons with women and children. He has never seen such a sight! Why are they here? What do they want? He quickly runs to warn the villagers working in the fields.

This map shows the main roads and forts in Roman Britain.

A Long Straight Road

The Romans came to Britain in AD 43 in search of metals such as tin, copper, silver and gold. Wherever they went, the Romans built forts with roads between so that they could move troops quickly. One of the most famous Roman roads, Watling Street, passes nearby, but not actually through, the Black Country. The Romans didn't discover the rich stores of iron that lay under the ground in the Black Country.

The people living in the Black Country when the Romans marched by were a Celtic tribe called the Cornovii. They had hill forts in the midlands and controlled the salt mines. They would get used to seeing Romans on their way somewhere else. One of the places the Romans might have been heading for was the city of Chester, or they might be troops moving up to build Emperor Hadrian's Wall to guard the northernmost limit of their Empire.

TUDOR
1485-1603

STUART
1603-1714

GEORGIAN
1714-1837

VICTORIAN
1837-1901

MODERN
TIMES
1902-NOW

Local Trade

A vital road such as Watling Street was defended by forts all along the route. Over time, these forts and staging posts became thriving little towns surrounded by wall and ditch defences. Where two roads crossed a lot of trade went on. The Black Country had four of these trading posts on its borders at Wall, Penkridge, Kingswinford and Edgbaston. The towns attracted traders from abroad, bringing pottery, metal, ornaments, glassware, wine and oil. Local Britons could exchange these imported goods for their farm produce such as vegetables, fruit, poultry, cheese and milk.

The Black Country didn't get its name until Victorian times.

A Roman-Briton family might have traded the farm produce for new and exciting things such as glass and olive oil.

By AD 410, the Roman army had left to defend Rome against barbarian invasions.

You can visit the remains of Letocetum at Wall, once an important transport hub that connected the Roman cities of Britain.

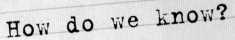

How do we know?

Archaeologists have learned a lot about the Romans from digging a site at Wall, near Lichfield. They have uncovered a Roman bathhouse and other buildings. It was a staging post for travellers and it provided a place to stay, and rest for horses. The other sites were near Penkridge, Kingswinford and Edgbaston, but the routes linking them together are completely lost.

SPOT THIS!

This is a statue of the Roman god Apollo, put up in 1939 – but where? Here's a clue: it's in Dudley's Coronation Gardens.

CELT
500 BC

ROMAN
AD 43-410

ANGLO-
SAXON
AD 450-
1066

VIKING
AD 865-
1066

MEDIE
TIM
1066-

Invaders

Longships come silently up the river at night. The westerly wind fills their square sails helping them row against the current. They are deep in enemy territory. Each boat is filled with men ready to plunder. The tiller man steers them upstream with an oar carved with the head of a dragon. This was how the Vikings liked to attack – with stealth and extreme violence.

0 25 50 75 100
Scale
(Kilometres)

N

Northumbria

Lindsey

East Anglia

(The Black Country)

Hwicca

Mercia

Essex

Wessex

Kent

Sussex

This map shows the kingdoms of Britain in Anglo-Saxon times. Can you see if some names have stayed the same?

The Battle of Tettenhall

The Vikings were fearless explorers from Scandinavia. They raided Britain stealing, killing anyone who tried to stop them, and taking the treasure back to their ships. But this time they were caught in a trap. On 5th August AD 910 a massive army was waiting for them. There were warriors hiding in the hills and forests near Tettenhall, and they attacked with fury. The Vikings tried to return to the safety of their ships, but their way was blocked. They were surrounded. They had no choice but to face their enemy in battle – and they lost.

Kingdom of Mercia

The victors at the Battle of Tettenhall were the Anglo-Saxons, people from Germany who had invaded and settled here after the Romans left. The Anglo-Saxons divided Angle-Land into small kingdoms, pushing the native Celts westwards. The Black Country was part of the Kingdom of Mercia.

The Black Country was a blanket of green forests and heath, crossed by rough tracks and dotted with tiny clearings. There were waterwheels on the rivers Tame and Stour to power flour mills, and forts such as the stronghold built by a Saxon ruler called 'Dudd', or 'Dodo', in Dudley.

TUDOR
1485-1603

STUART
1603-1714

GEORGIAN
1714-1837

VICTORIAN
1837-1901

MODERN
TIMES
1902-NOW

Lady Wulfruna

The Vikings were not put off by their defeat at Tettenhall. In AD 943 the Viking leader, Olaf Guthfrithson, led a fierce and bloody attack on Tamworth, which resulted in the capture of Wulfruna, a Saxon noblewomen. She held land and property in her own right on an equal basis to Saxon noblemen. She was also a member of the powerful Mercian ruling family. The Danish Vikings held her to ransom – Olaf knew that Wulfruna was important enough to extract a high price for her release. After, to give thanks, she founded the church in Wolverhampton, where her name is remembered to this day.

A statue of Lady Wulfruna stands outside St Peter's Church, Wolverhampton.

Country Life

The Vikings began settling around the Black Country. The old Roman road, Watling Street, became a boundary between Viking parts of England and the Anglo-Saxon kingdoms. The Anglo-Saxons became Christians and began to build simple churches, but the old Saxon and Norse gods are still remembered in the days of the week.

A hoard of Anglo-Saxon gold dug up in a field near Brownhills in 2009 is worth more than £1,000,000!

English	Saxon/Norse
Monday	Mona
Tuesday	Tiu
Wednesday	Woden
Thursday	Thor
Friday	Freya
Saturday	Sæternesdæg
Sunday	Sunne

The English days of the week are named after Saxon and Norse gods.

Hand over the Danegeld or you don't get Wulfruna back!

SPOT THIS!

This column is decorated with wild swirling designs carved by Saxons. Can you spot it? Here's a clue – it's not far from St Peter's Church in Wolverhampton.

Aisley is an Anglo-Saxon girl living in the Kingdom of Mercia. She is a serving girl of the noblewoman Wulfruna. This is an imaginary diary entry describing her day, though she would not have been able to read or write.

Everyone is talking about the Viking raids - it's very scary!

Thordag (Thursday)

This evening as I was fetching water from the stream, I heard shouts from the village. I hurried back to find a messenger had arrived from Tamworth. He'd run all the way to Heantune with terrible news! I set the water to boil while food and drink was laid out for him. We settled around the fire to listen to his news. He told us that Vikings raided the King's stronghold last night, setting light to buildings and stealing anything of value. But that was not the worst of it. They have taken the Lady Wulfruna! They seized her and took her off into the night!

The men talked on late into the night. They plan to dig a deeper ditch around the village tomorrow and make sure the wooden stockade is strong. My brother and little sister fell asleep, but I couldn't sleep for thinking about those Vikings. They are close by and getting closer. Surely King Edmund, king of all England, will save Lady Wulfruna. But what will become of us?

The Vikings settled alongside the Anglo-Saxons, attracted by the rich hunting forests and water mills of the Black Country.

The Vikings had writing like this. Can you write your name in Runes? →

a	b		d	e	f	g	h	i
jy		k	l	m		s	t	vw
z		eo	ng	th				

VIKING RUNES

Wulfruna's children grew up hating the Vikings but her grand-daughter married the Viking king Canute.

How do we know?

Monks and scribes kept a written record of England, year by year, called the Anglo-Saxon Chronicle. The Battle of Tettenhall on 5th August AD 910 is recorded there, and the record for the year AD 943 shows that Lady Wulfruna was kidnapped by Vikings, but it does not say how much ransom money had to be paid for her safe return.

If you met an Anglo-Saxon today you wouldn't understand a word he said, but most of the words we say come from their language. The Black Country word 'bostin' which means excellent or very good probably comes from the Old English word 'bogan', which meant 'bursting'. Here are some examples of place names that come from Anglo-Saxon.

WULFRUNA'S HEANTOWN — WOLVERHAMPTON
WODEN'S BURG — WEDNESBURY
WODEN'S FELD — WEDNESFIELD
HALH'S OWEN - HALESOWEN
HRYEG LEAH — BRIERLEY
CRADDER'S LEAH — CRADLEY
DUDDER'S LEAH — DUDLEY
WILLA'S HALH — WILLENHALL
WALS HALH — WALSALL

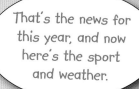

That's the news for this year, and now here's the sport and weather.

Copies of the Anglo-Saxon Chronicle were kept at monasteries where they were updated each year. This is a page of the Peterborough Chronicle.

CELT
500 BC

ROMAN
AD 43-410

ANGLO-
SAXON
AD 450-
1066

VIKING
AD 865-
1066

MEDIEV.
TIMES
1066-14

Castles and Manors

Wagons haul the rough stone slowly up the hill. The serfs unload the wagons and carry the stone to the stonemasons to be cut. The Norman soldiers shout commands – they are the masters now. The old timber fortifications are being taken down. Thick stone walls rise up slowly in their place. From the top of the unfinished walls you can see in all directions – from the quarry where the stones are being cut to the woods that are being felled to provide roof timbers. From up here the Normans will be able to control the land around.

The Dudley Estate

When the Normans attacked England in 1066, they won. William the Conqueror gave Dudley to one of his noblemen, William Fitz-Ansculf, in 1086. Fitz-Ansculf constructed earthworks for a castle: a vast mound of soil, or motte, surrounded by an earth bank, called a bailey, and ditch. The fort itself was built of wood. In return for Dudley, the baron had to keep an army of soldiers to fight for the king. So he gave part of his land to knights, who each commanded foot soldiers. The land was farmed by peasants, called serfs, who belonged to the baron. He could sell them if he wanted to.

But wooden forts were easily set alight by attackers. Fitz-Ansculf's son or grandson rebuilt the fort in stone once the earth motte had compacted enough to take their weight.

The castle keep was built on a soil mound called a motte, with timber fortifications. Stone walls were added 100 years later when the earth had settled enough to take their weight.

One, two, three, four oxen – add them to the Domesday list, Piers!

TUDOR
1485-1603

STUART
1603-1714

GEORGIAN
1714-1837

VICTORIAN
1837-1901

MODERN TIMES
1902-NOW

Manors and Mills

A later Lord of Dudley, Gervase Pagnell, built the priory of St James in 1160. It was a community of Benedictine monks attached to the Dudley estate. Other priories were founded in Halesowen and Sandwell. Most of daily life was centred around the Church, organizing work and looking after the sick. The priories kept huge flocks of sheep. Wool was sold abroad to be made into cloth. Wolverhampton became a wealthy town from the wool trade. Meanwhile in Walsall they made saddles and bridles out of leather.

The Monks Infirmary at Halesowen Abbey, built around 1218, is still standing on farmland near Halesowen.

The daily routine of a monk went from Lauds (morning prayers) to Compline (bedtime prayers).

Yippee, market day! We can sell more wool to buy socks.

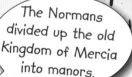
The Normans divided up the old kingdom of Mercia into manors.

SPOT THIS!

Can you spot the coffin of John de Somery, Lord of Dudley, in the undercroft of Dudley Castle?

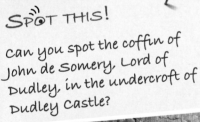

How do we know?

William the Conqueror wanted to know exactly what he had conquered. So the Domesday Book was compiled by scribes in 1086. It was a survey of the whole country, listing anything of value. As the scribes commented: "not an ox, a cow, a pig was left out". Many local places are mentioned in the Domesday Book, such as Smethwick, which was then a tiny hamlet called Smedeuuich.

You can still find evidence of the wool trade in the street names of Wolverhampton. There's Woolpack Street, Townwell Fold and Blossom's Fold. A woolpack was a bale of wool. A fold was a fenced enclosure where sheep were kept.

1220 WALSALL AND 1258 WOLVERHAMPTON HOLD MARKETS AND FAIRS...

CELT
500 BC

ROMAN
AD 43-410

ANGLO-
SAXON
AD 450-
1066

VIKING
AD 865-
1066

MEDIEV
TIME.
1066
1485

Tudor Troubles

The terrified abbot watches, helpless, as the king's men destroy his abbey. They take the precious coloured glass from windows and strip lead from the windows and roof. Even the wooden pews are being looted. A sudden clang from above tells the abbot that even the abbey bells are no longer safe. After standing for more than 300 years there will soon be nothing left but an empty ruin. The year is 1539 and the king, Henry VIII, has ordered the destruction of Halesowen Abbey.

Close down the monasteries, collect the treasure and sell off the land!

This drawing of Halesowen Abbey ruins was made by Elizabeth Reynolds in 1834.

Royal favours

When King Henry VIII argued with the Catholic Pope over his divorce from the queen, Catherine of Aragon, Henry made himself head of a new Church of England. He set about destroying the monasteries, which were run by Catholic monks loyal to the Pope. All three of the priories in the Black Country were destroyed, though the ruins at Dudley and Halesowen remain.

Nine years after Henry VIII died, his second daughter became Queen Elizabeth I. She was a Protestant but her cousin, Mary Queen of Scots, was Catholic. When Mary was suspected of plotting to take over the English throne she became a royal prisoner. Inspectors were sent to Dudley Castle but they declared it was not comfortable enough for Mary. When Queen Elizabeth visited Dudley Castle in 1575 she found it very comfortable, but then she was a royal guest, not a prisoner!

TUDOR
1485-1603

STUART
1603-1714

GEORGIAN
1714-1837

VICTORIAN
1837-1901

MODERN
TIMES
1902-NOW

Gunpowder Plot!

Religion became an important issue again when Elizabeth I died and James VI of Scotland became King James I of England. A Catholic, called Guy Fawkes, was arrested in a cellar trying to blow up the Houses of Parliament. His fellow plotters fled to a house in Himley, called Holbeache House. They were followed by the sheriff and his men, who soon had the house surrounded. They tried to make another escape but it was hopeless. In the shoot-out most of them were killed, and the others taken prisoner. But some may have escaped through a narrow tunnel hidden under the floor of Holbeche House which can still be seen today.

Remember, remember, the 5th of November, gunpowder, treason and plot!

SPOT THIS!

Holbeche House is near Kingswinford. Can you spot it? Here's a clue: it's now a nursing home.

We remember Guy Fawkes' Gunpowder Plot every 5th November with firework displays and bonfires.

Dud Dudley and Civil War

Dud Dudley took over the iron furnaces and forges at Pensnett Chase which his father, Lord Dudley, owned. He experimented with smelting iron ore using coal to improve the quality of the iron. The king granted a patent for his method in 1622 and Dudley opened another forge at Cradley. But the Mayday Flood of 1623 destroyed his ironworks and much of Cradley.

When the English Civil War broke out in 1642, forges at Stourbridge and Dudley were making shot and cannon for the Parliamentarians. Dud Dudley, a Colonel in Charles I's Royalist army, supplied the Royalists with muskets and carbines. But Dud Dudley was unlucky again – the Royalists lost the war and Cromwell's victorious army destroyed Dudley Castle.

My ironworks were swept away by the Mayday Flood.

This is an imaginary likeness of Dud Dudley, one of the first great ironmasters of the Black Country.

CELT
500 BC

ROMAN
AD 43-410

ANGLO-
SAXON
AD 450-
1066

VIKING
AD 865-
1066

MEDIEV
TIME.
1066
1485

Queen Elizabeth I toured the country to visit her supporters. In 1575 she came to stay at Dudley Castle, the home of Lord Edward Dudley. A lavish banquet would have been prepared for the royal visit. Here is an imaginary account from Anne, a 10-year-old serving girl, though she would not have been able to read or write.

The pie for the Queen's banquet was so enormous, they had to carry it to the table on a stretcher!

I have never been so busy in all my life, running about the castle fetching things and carrying messages. At last Her Majesty arrived by carriage, accompanied by men on horse and many wagons. Her Majesty was met by his Lordship, who bowed so low I thought he would never get up again!

Me and the other serving girls stood on both sides of the grand staircase in our new white dresses holding out little baskets of white petals. As the Queen passed, we curtsied and sprinkled petals under her feet. I peeped up as she passed —she was tall, fair and her clothes glittered with gold and pearls!

Tonight, the Great Hall was lit up by torches along the walls. At the centre of the long banqueting table was an enormous pie, in the shape of a crown. The kitchen boy told me that this pie contained a whole deer, a gosling, three capons, six chickens, ten pigeons and one rabbit! Any gaps were filled with minced veal and twenty-six hard-boiled eggs, coloured with saffron and flavoured with cloves.

Everyone had to take sides in the violent power struggles between church, crown and parliament.

To Bake Red Deere

Parboyl it, and then sauce it in Vinegar then Lard it very thick, and season it with Pepper, Ginger and Nutmegs, put it into a deep Pye with good store of sweet butter, and let it bake, when it is baked, take a pint of Hippocras, halfe a pound of sweet butter, two or three Nutmeg, little Vinegar, poure it into the Pye in the Oven and let it lye and soake an hour, then take it out, and when it is cold stop the vent hole.

TUDOR
1485-1603

STUART
1603-1714

GEORGIAN
1714-1837

VICTORIAN
1837-1901

MODERN
TIMES
1902-NOW

1575
Bur. John Waynewright, Mar. 26th.
Chr. Richard Parker, Elizabeth Parsus and
    Adam Downing, Mar. 27th.
Bur. Elizabeth Whithouse, Mar. 28th.
Chr. John Hickmans, Apr. 8th.
Chr. Margarett Ap. Owen, Apr. 18th.
Chr. John Houghton, Apr. 24th.
Bur. Alice Whithouse, Apr. 26th.
Chr. Margery Aderley, May 15th.
Chr. Thomas Houghton and
    Elizabeth Wilks, May 24th.
Bur. Thomas Tornor (no date entered)
Bur. Thomas Parsus of Turlus Hill, July 2nd.
Chr. Christian Wildsmith, July 17th.
Chr. John Pearson, July 24th.
Chr. Anne Tymmings, Aug. 14th.
Chr. Richard Tymmings, Aug. 21st.
Chr. Mary Hall, Aug. 24th.
Bur. Francis Dunsterfild, Sept. 8th.
Bur. Margarett Aderley, Sept. 17th.
Chr. Marjorie Hickmans and
    Agnes Gibbins, Sept. 18th.
Bur. John Hickmans, Sept. 27th.
Chr. Phillip Marall, Sept. 30th.
Chr. Ellin Cook, Nov. 6th.
Bur. Elizabeth Nock, Nov. 7th.
Chr. Aleyander Corbet, Nov. 20th.
Bur. Elizabeth Tymmings, Nov. 26th.
Bur. Thomas Barnes, Dec. 18th.

Oak House Museum in West Bromwich shows what life was like in a grand Tudor house.

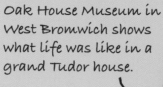

A page from Sedgley parish register 1575, the year Elizabeth I came to the Black Country.

Foreign ambassadors at Elizabeth I's court describe her as tall, fair, graceful, clever but with big hands!

How do we know?

In 1665, Dud Dudley wrote about the process of smelting iron ore in a book called 'Metallum Martis'. In it, he drew a map of Dudley Castle showing the layers of coal and iron ore. This is one of the earliest geology maps.

Old parish churches, like the one at Sedgley, kept a register of births, marriages and deaths going back to Tudor times. They recorded the jobs people did and how many children they had. As time went on, there were fewer farmers or Yeomen and more nail-makers and foundrymen – showing how industry was growing.

What was actually served on the night of Queen Elizabeth's visit is long forgotten, but recipes from books written at the time give us an idea of what might have been prepared.

There are many portraits of Elizabeth I painted at the time, so we should know what she looked like. But some artists made her look prettier and younger to keep on her good side!

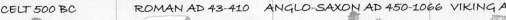

Industrial Revolution

Joseph shakes the horse's reins. "Come on, my Beauty, not far now." The air is cool and crisp after the dark stale air of the Dudley Tunnel. Wisps of mist are beginning to rise from the water. The horse slowly plods along the towpath, pulling the heavy canal barge, with its load of limestone from Wren's Nest. It's been a long, tiring day but their destination is now within reach. They'll wait until tomorrow before tackling the nine sections of the Delph Locks.

Toll keepers collected payments from boats and barges passing through the locks.

Telford's Galton Bridge near Smethwick has a single span of 46 metres. It was the highest single span bridge in the world when it was built in 1829.

Canals

Canals were the motorways of the 1700s, transporting heavy limestone and coal to the growing number of factories around the Midlands. Limestone was needed to make iron and the smelting process needed furnaces, burning tons of coal, and the Black Country had plenty of both. Soon there were quarries and mines everywhere and the population of the Black Country soared.

James Brindley built the Birmingham Canal from Wolverhampton to Birmingham in 1768–1772. The canal was so successful that there were soon traffic jams. By 1827, Thomas Telford had built the New Main Line cutting the journey between Birmingham and Wolverhampton by a third.

Canals had to be level. Aqueducts, such as Galton Bridge, were built to carry the canal over a valley. Locks, such as the famous nine Delph Locks, at Brierley Hill, were built to raise and lower barges up and down slopes.

Steam Engines

The first steam engines ever built were used to pump water out of mines. Thomas Newcomen built the first steam engine in 1712 and installed it in the Conygree Coalworks near Dudley.

The Smethwick Steam Engine, built in 1779 to supply water to operate the locks at Smethwick, is now housed at the Thinktank Science Museum in Birmingham. It is the oldest working engine in the world!

Soon the power of steam was used in locomotives – railway transport was quicker than the canals. In the Black Country the railways were not for passengers but for heavy goods – short stretches of line connected the coal mines with the factories. Tipton had seven train stations, all busy taking deliveries of limestone and coal or loading up trucks with iron, leather goods or precious glassware.

> You can see a replica of the Newcomen Steam Engine at the Black Country Living Museum, Dudley.

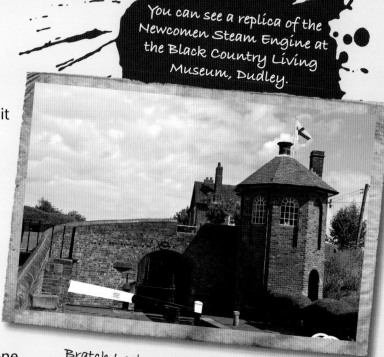

Bratch Lock and Toll House at Wombourne were opened in 1772.

Glass-making

Glass was rare and expensive. Most people did not have glass in their windows – on a cold day you shut the shutters and sat in the dark. French exiles, called Huguenots, had settled in Brierley Hill and Stourbridge, bringing their glass-making skills to the area. Canals, and later railways, were perfect for transporting things made from glass because it was much smoother travelling on water than along bumpy roads!

> Coal and iron from the Black Country powered the industrial revolution.

The Red House Glass Cone is now museum. Glass has been made here since about 1790.

SPOT THIS!

John Northwood was famous for his glass carving. This statue of him stands in the Merry Wood Shopping Centre near Brierley Hill.

This is the imaginary story of Benjamin, a 10-year-old boy working on the canals in the Black Country. After working their way through the locks, they came to Castle Hill at Dudley. Here the horse pulling the canal barge was unhitched and taken round the hill, whilst the boat went under it – through a tunnel.

> Dudley Tunnel is the worst – it's 2,900 metres long – the second longest in England!

Tuesday 4th May 1790

We were legging through the tunnel…you know what legging is? If you have never done it I can tell you what it's like: it's horrible! Lord Dudley won't let us use boathooks, he says they scratch away the precious brickwork of his tunnels, so we have to lie down on the top of the barge and use our feet like upturned beetles. It is hard work, pulling the barge along with your feet. Your legs ache…your back aches…

Under Castle Hill there is a giant cave where they have been cutting out the limestone, and there's a basin where boats can be loaded up. It feels like you are in a goblin's mountain hall. The men loaded our barge with limestone and then one of them put down his shovel and took out a lump of stone from his pocket, wrapped in the paper he must have had his lunch in.

"Here, grab this, it'll make you a few pennies," he said.

As soon as we were in the long tunnel I climbed up onto the roof and as I legged I opened up the greasy paper. In the darkness I felt a smooth spiral shape with my fingers. I grinned. It was a good one. I slipped it into my bag. You see, Lord Dudley doesn't like us taking out fossils.

> A single strong horse could pull 50 tonnes by canal boat.

How do we know?

At the Black Country Living Museum you can still see the old boatyards and boats. You can even take a boat to the limestone quarries yourself.

Everyday life went by unrecorded, but accidents made the newspapers, which is how we know about the Nine Locks Ordeal of 1869. Thirteen miners were trapped in a flooded mine shaft. It took almost a week for the water to be pumped out so they could be rescued. They were so hungry they ate their candles and had to sit in the dark. They even tried eating coal and shoelaces! The twelve survivors were local heroes.

There were so many mineshafts being dug it was impossible to keep track of them all. You never know when you are standing on a disused mine, until it collapses and you fall down a hole! So tread carefully.

This statue in Tipton is of William Perry, who as a boy worked on the canals. He became a professional prize fighter and by 1850 was the champion of England.

The Dudley Bug is the fossil of a trilobite, a sea creature that lived over 450 million years ago.

'Leggers' were employed at Dudley Tunnel to walk the boat through.

19

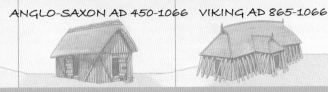

A Royal Visitor

The train chunters onwards through the forest of factory chimneys belching smoke. It is 30th November, 1866 and this is Queen Victoria's first outing since the death of her dear husband, Prince Albert. She is coming to unveil a bronze statue of him in the main square of Wolverhampton, renamed Queen Square in her honour. When she gets off the train she is led through cheering crowds under an archway cut out of an enormous slab of coal.

I am Queen of the United Kingdom of Britain and Ireland and Empress of India.

The picture shows children carrying clay to make bricks in 1871.

Child Labour

When Queen Victoria came to the throne in 1837, there were thousands of small factories in the Black Country. Guns were made in Darlaston, locks in Willenhall, leather goods in Walsall and chains in Netherton and Cradley Heath. But working conditions were harsh, and children as young as four worked.

In the smallest factories a family worked together in a shed. Nail-makers had a coil of wire delivered to the cottage. It was cut into lengths and hammered to a point one end and to a flat head on the other end. The family was paid by the number of nails they made. They had to work at least 10 hours a day to feed the family. Small family workshops around Wolverhampton and Bilston produced painted tin goods using a technique called japaning.

While Queen Victoria was on the throne, three laws were passed making work safer and hours shorter, and raising the age when you could start work. By 1878, no child under 10 could work in a factory or mine, or for more than 10 hours a day.

Poverty and Sickness

You look like you could do with a good wash!

Not likely, Miss!

The deadly disease cholera killed hundreds of people in 1832 and again in 1849. Churchyards were full and had to be closed. The nearest hospital was a bumpy cart-ride away in Birmingham. The main cause of disease was overcrowding in the towns. Filthy water lay in the streets or drained into the local river. Scavengers were employed to collect night soil and clean the streets.

Things began to improve in the Black Country. The Walsall Union Workhouse opened in 1838 to provide work and shelter for the homeless poor. Walsall Cottage Hospital opened on Bridge Street. A nurse called Dorothy Pattison arrived to work here during a smallpox epidemic in 1875. She later became known as Sister Dora. By 1895 new underground drains carried away the sewage and Bratch Pumping Station was bringing clean drinking water to Wolverhampton.

New open spaces, such as Victoria Park in Smethwick, provided fresh air and exercise away from the smog and smoke of the factories.

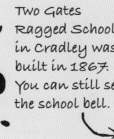

The first US steam train, the 'Stourbridge Lion', was built by Foster, Rastrick and Company in 1829 and shipped across the Atlantic Ocean to Pennsylvania.

Two Gates Ragged School in Cradley was built in 1867. You can still see the school bell.

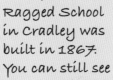

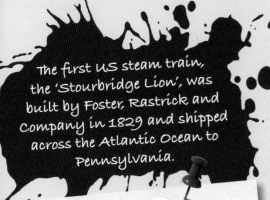

School

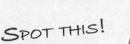

SPOT THIS!

Can you spot this statue of Sister Dora in Walsall. Here's a clue: look near the Bridge.

At the beginning of Victorian times, it was mostly wealthy children who went to school. Some poor children were lucky enough to go to charity schools such as the Two Gates Ragged School in Cradley. In 1878 a law was passed saying that all children between the ages of 5 and 10 had to go to school. At 7 years old, girls and boys went into school through separate entrances and had separate playgrounds. The children were taught the three 'Rs' – reading, writing and arithmetic. They also learned poems such as 'The Charge of the Light Brigade' by Alfred Lord Tennyson. Swords and cannon used in the Crimean War would have been made by their fathers working in the iron forges.

Every school in Wolverhampton was closed in honour of the royal visit, but the children had to work extra hard the next day, writing an essay on what they had done. Here is an imaginary essay written by 8-year-old Tommy who went with his sister Mary.

30th November 1866

It was biting cold this morning when we went down to Railway Street. There were barriers to stop us going onto the road, but my sister lifted me up to see over the top. We waited for hours in the crowd, but it was worth it. When the train arrived at the station we saw the Queen get into her carriage, and everyone cheered. Next I saw the Prince and Princess getting in another carriage. I waved so hard I thought my arm would fall off! Mary said the best bit was seeing the Princess wave, but I thought the best bit was getting a bun! I got a medal with a picture of the Queen on it which I will keep forever to remind me of the day.

If Her Majesty walks past us, you bow and I'll curtsy.

The Illustrated London News reported Queen Victoria's visit to Wolverhampton. It was the first royal visit the Queen had made since her husband, Prince Albert, had died.

Llewellyn Edwards was awarded a certificate on 24th August 1877 for Regular Attendance at Bank Street Board School, Brierley Hill.

'Black by day and red by night.' That's how the Black Country looked in 1862 and how it got its name.

How do we know?

The National Census collected information about people living all over Britain every ten years. The census records the name, age, occupation and place of birth of each member of the household.

The day Queen Victoria came to Wolverhampton was very special for schoolchildren who joined in a procession. School records tell us that children were given a medal and a bun.

First-hand accounts survive of Sister Dora's work at Walsall Cottage Hospital, especially during the smallpox epidemic of 1875.

Passenger railways had become very popular by the 1880s. The Halesowen and Northfield line took passengers to work at the new Austin factory at Longbridge.

Glass was supplied for the Crystal Palace in 1851 and the clock face of Big Ben in London by the Chance Brothers of Smethwick.

You can find out more about Sister Dora at Walsall Museum. They even have a lock of her hair.

CELT
500 BC

ROMAN
AD 43-410

ANGLO-
SAXON
AD 450-
1066

VIKING
AD 865-
1066

MEDIE
TIM
1066-

Newcomers

There is great excitement. Dudley has never seen a building anything like this before, with its wavy peppermint-green roof and huge letters spelling out Z-O-O. It is 18th May, 1937. A queue stretches all the way to The Broadway. People from miles around have come to see the most modern zoo in the world. There are no bars on the enclosures. We will be face to face with exotic animals we have only ever seen in books. There is even a penguin pool! The heaving crowd presses against the gates. Will we ever get inside?

When Dudley Zoo first opened it housed 3,000 animals and birds!

At War

After World War One, the Earl of Dudley had to find a way to pay for the upkeep of the Castle. He asked the modern achitect Lubetkin to design a zoo for him. It was an instant success. But two years later, World War Two began. As Dudley's men went off to fight, the women stepped in to take care of the animals. Women worked in the factories, too. Factories making trucks and saucepans began making parts for tanks, bombs and ammunition. The Black Country was busier than ever.

Perhaps because there wasn't one big target for the bombers, the Black Country wasn't blitzed as London and nearby Coventry were. Children were evacuated to the area from the cities for safety. Some of them stayed in Haden Hill House, a rambling Victorian mansion built beside Haden Hall in Cradley Heath.

Haden Hall, in Cradley Heath, was built in Tudor times. A new house was built in the 1870s next to the old house. Some people believe the old house is haunted.

TUDOR
1485-1603

STUART
1603-1714

GEORGIAN
1714-1837

VICTORIAN
1837-1901

MODERN
TIMES
1902-NOW

Rebuilding

There was a lot of work to do rebuilding the country after the war. There was a shortage of workers in Britain and people were encouraged to come here from the British Commonwealth countries. People from the Caribbean, India and Pakistan settled in the Black Country. But in the 1960s and 1970s the coal mines and then the iron works closed as cheap imports were brought in from abroad. There were not so many jobs as people supposed. Men and women from all backgrounds lost their jobs and it took time for work opportunities to improve.

In December 1982, the Round Oak Steelworks in Brierley Hill, started by the Earl of Dudley in 1857, closed putting thousands of people out of work. As industries closed so did some of the rail networks that linked them. The Black Country had to reinvent itself. In the 1980s the Merry Hill Shopping Centre was built on the old Round Oak site creating thousands of new jobs. The Chubb factory building was converted into the Light House Media Centre.

In 1910, Noah Hingley and Sons Ltd of Netherton manufactured the massive anchor chains for RMS Titanic, the largest passenger steamship in the world.

Chubb Locks supplied locks for Her Majesty's prisons.

SPOT THIS!

The coal mines have gone, but there are still old mine shafts beneath the Black Country. Can you spot 'The Crooked House' which began to sink when the mines beneath it collapsed? Here's a clue: try Wolverhampton.

After the war, people from the British Commonwealth came to help rebuild the country.

New Beginning

Today the canals which once carried the industrial wealth of the Black Country now bring holiday-makers. The new Midland Metro light railway provides a fast link between Wolverhampton and Birmingham bringing visitors to Dudley Zoo and the Black Country Museum.

This is the imaginary diary of George, a Black Country schoolboy whose father is in the Royal Air Force. His father has been given 14 days' embarkation leave, which means he'll be posted overseas when he goes back.

Have you got your pencil, rubber, ruler, gas mask?

Dad's home! He's on embarkation leave. Mom says we'll make a fuss of him for the two weeks he's home before he goes away again.

Today I couldn't wait to get to school to show my friends what Dad gave me. He brought me a bit of perspex from the window of an airplane that came down. It's really thick. Everyone wanted to touch it. It's not sharp or cold like glass. Then there was an air raid and we had to go down into the boiler room with our gas masks. When the all clear sounded we had to start our lessons again, but I was thinking about my precious treasure.

Tonight we had rabbit stew for our tea. Dad had to skin the rabbit because Mom wouldn't touch it. It was the best meal we had in ages, much better than the meat ration. Dad wouldn't say where he got the rabbit from – he just winked at me. Then we heard the drone of airplanes going overhead and I thought Oh no, another raid! But Dad stepped out into the yard, listened for a moment, and said 'Ours.' What a relief!

Now I am going to bed. Dad's blue uniform is hanging on the back of the door, as if he is keeping guard over me.

Even animals wore gas masks. →

Keep calm and carry on!

News of the call-up for National Service in the Armed Forces was delivered to the door by telegram.

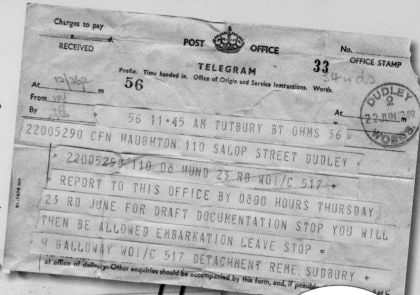

How do we know?

It is difficult to keep track of everyone in the chaos of war. Able-bodied men (fit to fight) were called up for the army, navy and airforce. Children from the bigger cities, such as Birmingham and Coventry, were evacuated with their teachers to the countryside for safety. They had labels tied to them, like luggage, so that they wouldn't get lost!

At the end of the war everyone had a story to tell. These stories are still being collected today, to go along with the history of battles lost and won. Here in the Black Country, with bombs falling and shortages of food, everyday life was so tough they called it the Home Front. But there were films and posters to encourage everyone to keep going.

Ration books, call-up telegrams and diaries all help us to build up a picture of what life was like during the war.

Dudley Zoo grew its own hay and vegetables to feed the animals.

DIG FOR VICTORY

27

CELT
500 BC

ROMAN
AD 43-410

ANGLO-
SAXON
AD 450-
1066

VIKING
AD 865-
1066

MEDI
TIM
1066-

The Black Country Today and Tomorrow

The Black Country's history can be discovered all around you. March up the hill to Dudley Castle, explore the Black Country Living Museum. The important thing to remember is that the Black Country's history is about the people who lived through difficult or exciting or dangerous times – children such as Aisley, Anne, Tommy, Mary, Benjamin and George!

Some Midland Metro trams are named after local people, such as number 05 - Sister Dora. Do you know someone who should have a tram named after them?

Today there are more than 1,500 animals at Dudley Zoo Gardens. Will the zoos of the future have the same animals on show?

The Black Country's Bostin!

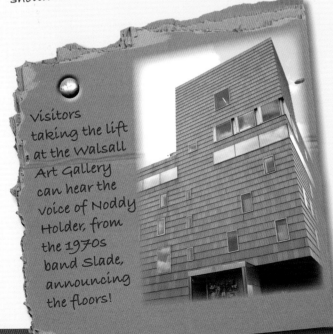

Visitors taking the lift at the Walsall Art Gallery can hear the voice of Noddy Holder, from the 1970s band Slade, announcing the floors!

Farley Clock Tower is a memorial to Reuben Farley, the first mayor of West Bromwich. What monuments do you think we will build and who do you think we should commemorate in the Black Country?

I'm going to capture this moment for all time!

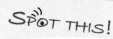

West Bromwich Albion has a proud history going back to 1878. What does the future hold for the Baggies?

Chubb's Lock Works once employed over 1,000 people making locks. Now it is home to the Light House Media Centre.

Broadfield House is a great place to see glass products from the Black Country and around the world.

How will they know?

Will the Black Country always look the way it does today? How will future generations know what it was like to live now? The Internet is a great way of recording what life is like today. Photos, blogs and stories from tourists can all spread the word about our wonderful Black Country. Or maybe you'll be famous one day and put the Black Country on the map!

The largest South Indian temple in Europe brings together the Hindu community from all over the Black Country.

Glossary

Abbey – where monks or nuns live and work. An abbot is in charge of the monks, an abbess is in charge of the nuns.

AD – a short way of writing the Latin words anno Domini, which mean 'in the year of our Lord', i.e. after the birth of Christ.

Air raid – during World War Two, enemy planes bombed Britain. This was called an air raid. A siren sounded to warn people of an air raid.

All clear – when an air raid was over, and it was safe again, another siren sounded, called the All Clear.

Archaeologist – a person who studies the past by examining buildings and objects left behind by people and cultures.

Catholic – also called Roman Catholic: member of a Christian religion, headed by the Pope.

Church of England – the Christian church in England that is headed by the king or queen.

Civil war – a war where people living in the same country fight each other.

Domesday Book – William the Conqueror sent men out to check who owned all the land and wealth in England. The results were written in the Domesday Book, which survives today.

Evacuate – leaving your home to live somewhere else for safety.

Gas mask – used in World War Two, this mask stopped you breathing poisonous gas.

Hadrian's Wall – a wall the Roman Emperor Hadrian had built across Northern England to keep out the North British tribes. Some of the wall still survives.

Hindu – a person who follows the Indian religion of Hinduism, which believes in many gods, especially Brahma.

Huguenot – a member of an old French Protestant religion.

Keep – the main tower within the walls of a castle or fortress.

Monk – a male member of a religious community that has rules of poverty, chastity and obedience.

Musket – a long-barrelled gun, loaded from the front, used from the 16th to the 18th centuries.

Parliamentarian – anyone who fought on the side of Oliver Cromwell and Parliament in the English Civil War.

Protestant – a member of the Christian religion who considers the king or queen to be the head of its church.

Ration book – during World War Two, some foods were rationed. Your ration book showed how much of this food you could have each week.

Royalist – anyone who fought on the side of King Charles I in the English Civil War.

Scavenger – someone who goes looking for things other people have thrown away.

Scribe – a person who made hand-written copies of books, before printing was invented.

Stonemason – someone who works with, and makes things from, stone.

Telegram – before everyone had telephones, urgent messages were delivered by the post office.

Index

Acknowledgements

To Nedra
The author and publishers would like to thank the following people for their generous help:
Jenni L James Black Country Genealogy and Family History

The publishers would like to thank the following people and organizations
for their permission to reproduce material on the following pages:
p5: Oosoom at en.wikipedia;
p9: Bodleian; Library, University of Oxford MS. Laud. Misc. 636, fol. 1r
p10: Dudley Castle;
p11: Dudley Castle;
p12: Sandwell Community History & Archives Service;
p13: Pictorial Press Ltd/Alamy;
p18: Dudley Museum & Art Gallery;
p19: Getty Images;
p20: The Print Collector/Alamy;
p22: Illustrated London News Ltd/Mary Evans;
p23: Black Country Genealogy and Family History, collection of Malvern Industrial Archaeology Circle;
p25: Jim Hicks of Portland, Oregon, USA and www.cradleylinks.co.uk;
p27: Black Country Genealogy & Family History

All other images copyright of Hometown World

Written by Edmund Bealby-Wright
Educational consultant: Neil Thompson
Local history consultant: Dr Malcolm Dick
Designed by Stephen Prosser

Illustrated by Kate Davies, Dynamo Ltd, Virginia Grey, Tim Hutchinson, Peter Kent, John MacGregor,
Leighton Noyes, Nick Shewring, Tim Sutcliffe and Victor Mclindon
Additional photographs by Alex Long

First published by HOMETOWN WORLD in 2011
Hometown World Ltd
7 Northumberland Buildings
Bath BA1 2JB

www.hometownworld.co.uk

hb ISBN 978-1-84993-011-6
pb ISBN 978-1-84993-146-5